Portly Potbellied Pigs

Alex Kuskowski
AUTHOR

C.A. Nobens
ILLUSTRATOR

Consulting Editor, Diane Craig, M.A./Reading Specialist

A Division of ABDO
ABDO
Publishing Company

visit us at www.abdopublishing.com

Published by ABDO Publishing Company, a division of ABDO, P.O. Box 398166, Minneapolis, Minnesota 55439. Copyright © 2013 by Abdo Consulting Group, Inc. International copyrights reserved in all countries. No part of this book may be reproduced in any form without written permission from the publisher. SandCastle™ is a trademark and logo of ABDO Publishing Company.

Printed in the United States of America, North Mankato, Minnesota
102012
012013

 PRINTED ON RECYCLED PAPER

Editor: Liz Salzmann
Content Developer: Nancy Tuminelly
Cover and Interior Design and Production: Kelly Doudna, Mighty Media, Inc.
Photo Credits: Ross Heywood, iStockPhoto (picturistic), Shutterstock

Library of Congress Cataloging-in-Publication Data

Kuskowski, Alex.
  Portly potbellied pigs / by Alex Kuskowski ; illustrator C.A. Nobens.
    p. cm. -- (Unusual pets)
  ISBN 978-1-61783-401-1
  1. Potbellied pigs as pets--Juvenile literature. I. Nobens, C. A., ill. II. Title.
  SF393.P74K87 2013
  636.4'0887--dc23
                        2011050812

SandCastle™ Level: Transitional

SandCastle™ books are created by a team of professional educators, reading specialists, and content developers around five essential components—phonemic awareness, phonics, vocabulary, text comprehension, and fluency—to assist young readers as they develop reading skills and strategies and increase their general knowledge. All books are written, reviewed, and leveled for guided reading, early reading intervention, and Accelerated Reader® programs for use in shared, guided, and independent reading and writing activities to support a balanced approach to literacy instruction. The SandCastle™ series has four levels that correspond to early literacy development. The levels are provided to help teachers and parents select appropriate books for young readers.

| Emerging Readers (no flags) | Beginning Readers (1 flag) | Transitional Readers (2 flags) | Fluent Readers (3 flags) |

Contents

Unusual Pets

Unusual pets can be interesting and fun! Unusual pets might also eat unusual food. They might have special care needs. It is a good idea to learn about your new friend before bringing it home.

There are special laws for many unusual animals. Make sure the kind of pet you want is allowed in your city and state.

Potbellied Pig Basics

Type of animal

Potbellied pigs are **mammals**.

Adult size

60 to 200 pounds (27 to 90 kg)

Life expectancy

10 to 15 years

Natural habitat

fields of
Southeastern
Asia

Potbellied pigs eat vegetables, meat, and fruit. Today, Josie feeds her pig apples.

Potbellied pigs need to spend time outside. Amber's piglet plays in the fresh grass.

Potbellied pigs love attention. Danielle plays with her pig after school.

Potbellied pigs have very good noses. They use them to **sniff** out treats.

A Potbellied Pig Story

My **cousin** lives in Idaho
and his name is Ziggy.
He's very proud of his pet,
a pig that he named Piggy!

Piggy is a clever **swine**.
She can do most anything.
She can dance and she can add.
She jumps right through a ring!

They have entered a talent show.
It is happening next week.
Ziggy is teaching Piggy
to kiss him on the cheek!

Every day they practice.
They really want to win.
The **trophy** is the largest
that it has ever been.

Ziggy is surprised
on the day of the big show.
In walks Stephanie Smith
with a skating crocodile in tow!

Ziggy waits for his turn.
He sees the croc skate past.
Those two are really great.
Can he and Piggy last?

Finally it's Piggy's turn.
People clap and cheer out loud.
Piggy runs around and dances.
She even paints some clouds!

The **competition** is very close.
The judges can't decide.
Then they say that Piggy won!
Ziggy beams with pride!

Fun Facts

* Pigs have no body odor.

* Most pigs have stiff hairs along their backs. They stick up when the pigs are happy or upset.

* People have been raising pigs for more than 10,000 years.

* Potbellied pigs were first brought to North America in the 1980s.

Potbellied Pig Quiz

Read each sentence below. Then decide whether it is true or false!

1. Pigs don't eat vegetables.

2. Potbellied pigs should never go outside.

3. Potbellied pigs love attention.

4. Piggy is a clever **swine**.

5. Ziggy and Piggy got second place at the talent show.

Answers: 1. False 2. False 3. True 4. True 5. False

Glossary

awe – a feeling of wonder and respect.

competition – a contest.

cousin – the child of your aunt or uncle.

mammal – a warm-blooded animal that has hair and whose females produce milk to feed their young.

sniff – to smell something.

swine – a hog or pig.

trophy – a prize given to the winner of a competition.